Exploring Space

Emily Kington

Contents

Words that appear in **bold** are explained in the glossary

Discover more at **www.hungrytomato.com**

Exploring Space

Space travel is still a very new science. It's been less than 100 years since the first spacecraft left **Earth's atmosphere**. There is still so much for us to explore and discover!

Animals were sent into space before humans, to see if it was safe to travel.

A Russian dog, named *Laika*, was the first animal to completely **orbit** the Earth in 1957. This statue in Moscow celebrates her important achievement.

The first human in space was Soviet **cosmonaut**, *Yuri Gagarin*. On 12 April 1961, he completed one orbit of Earth in the spacecraft *Vostok 1*.

More than 5,000 spacecraft have been launched into space since 1957.

Spacecraft

A spacecraft is a vehicle or machine designed to travel into outer space. They are used for lots of different things, including collecting information, exploring planets, and transport.

Building a spacecraft is very complicated. It can take up to 10 years to get one ready to launch.

A *lander* is a type of spacecraft that is designed to land on the surface of a planet or moon.

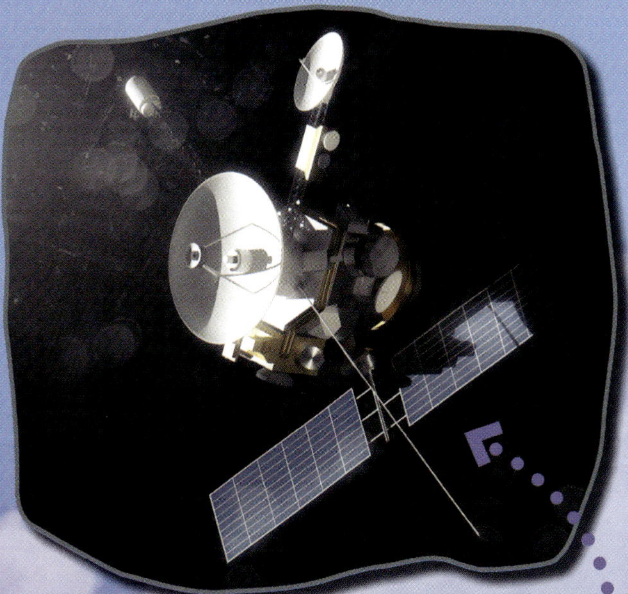

Space probes are robotic spacecraft that don't orbit Earth, but explore further out into space instead.

Space shuttles were the first reusable spacecraft and were used to carry crew and **cargo** on 135 missions between 1981 and 2011, when they were **retired**.

Lift-Off!

During the countdown, scientists at mission control, do final checks to make sure everything is working and that it is safe to launch.

Spacecraft and rockets are not the same thing. A rocket is used to carry a spacecraft outside of Earth's atmosphere.

Rockets carrying spacecraft usually take off from *launch pads* at a *spaceport*.

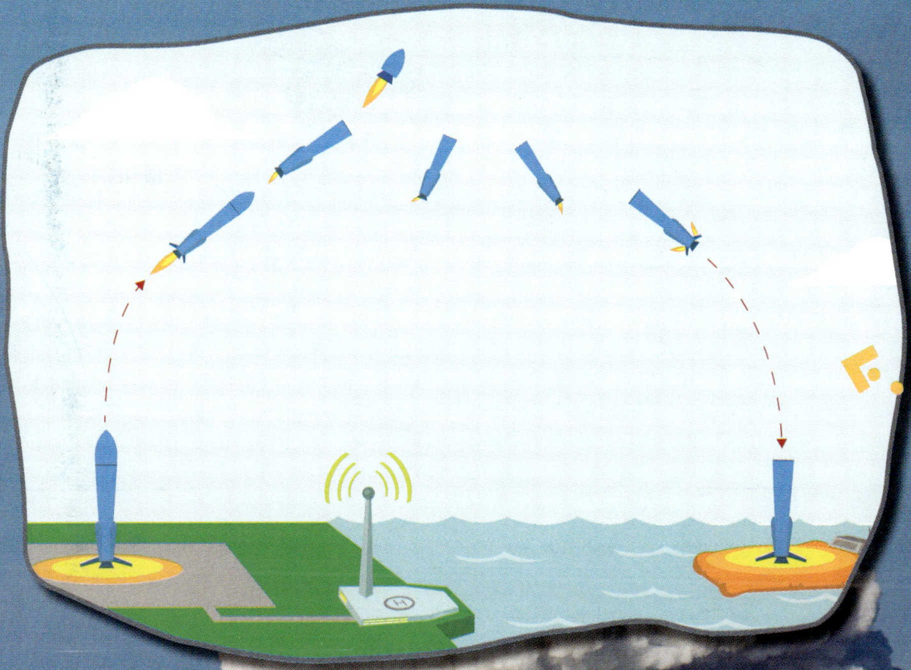

After launching, parts of the rocket that are no longer needed for travel, fall away in stages.

Rockets aren't just for space. The first rockets we know about were used as fireworks in 1200s, in China.

Race to the Moon

During the 1960s the race was on between the USA and Russia, as they competed to be the first country to send humans to the Moon.

Soviet spacecraft *Luna* 9 was the first vehicle to land on the Moon, in 1966. It took lots of photographs.

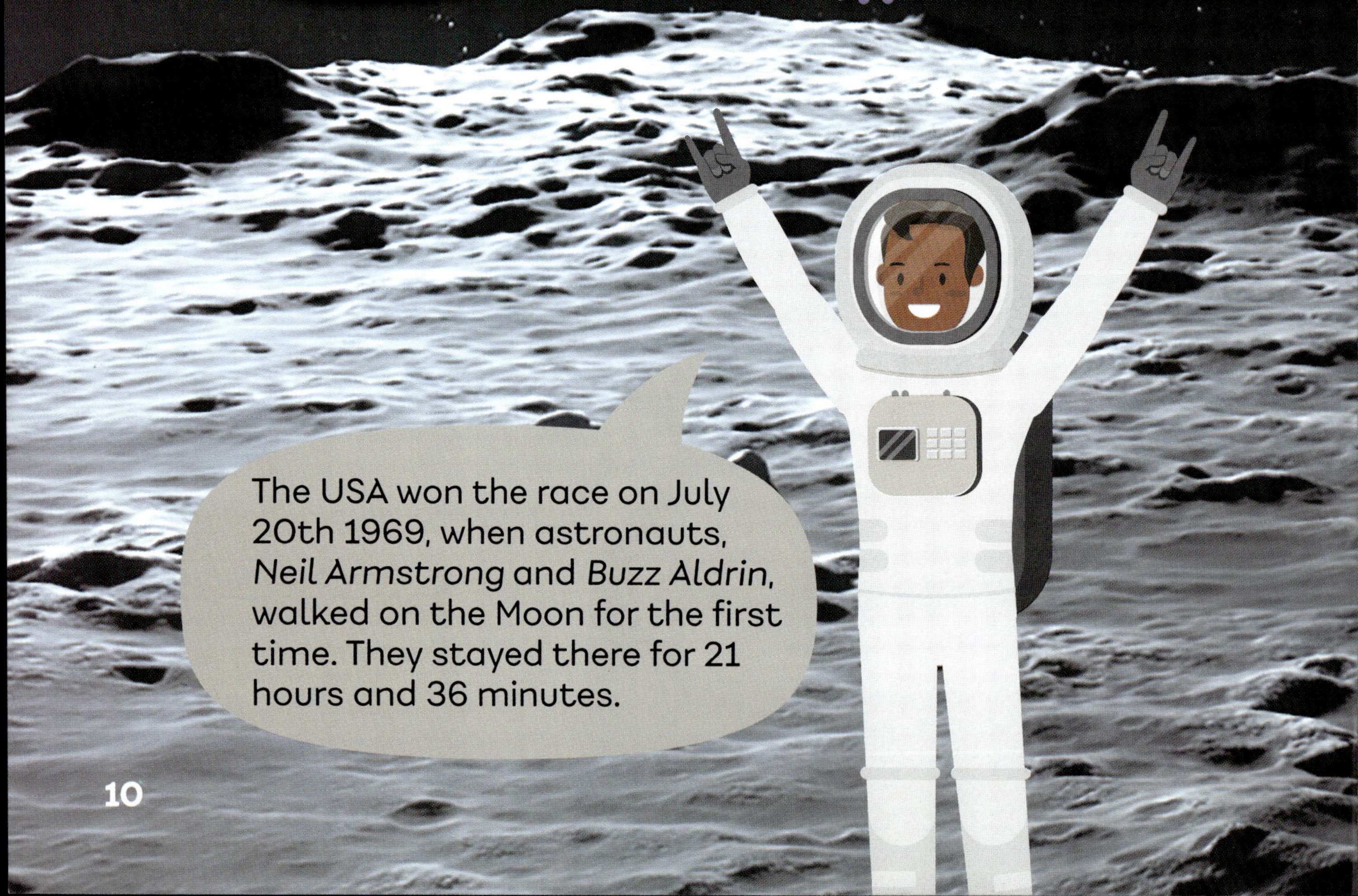

The USA won the race on July 20th 1969, when astronauts, *Neil Armstrong* and *Buzz Aldrin*, walked on the Moon for the first time. They stayed there for 21 hours and 36 minutes.

The first footprints will probably still be there, as there is no wind on the Moon to make them disappear.

Lunar Roving Vehicles (moon buggies) were taken to the Moon on later US missions for astronauts to travel in. They are still on the Moon, and belong to NASA.

Missions to Mars

Robotic spacecraft began observing Mars in the 1960s, looking for signs of life. No humans have visited Mars...yet!

Launches can only take place every two years when Mars is closer to Earth (35 million miles/56 million km). It takes a lot of rocket fuel to reach Mars!

A number of martian rocks (**meteorites** from Mars) have fallen to Earth, so scientists have been able to study Mars without leaving our planet!

Mars Rovers are robotic vehicles that have been sent to Mars to send back data and images.

On July 30th 2020, Mars rover *Perseverance* was launched. Its mission is to seek signs of ancient life and collect rock samples. It can't return samples to Earth itself, so another spacecraft will have to be built to collect them.

Telescopes

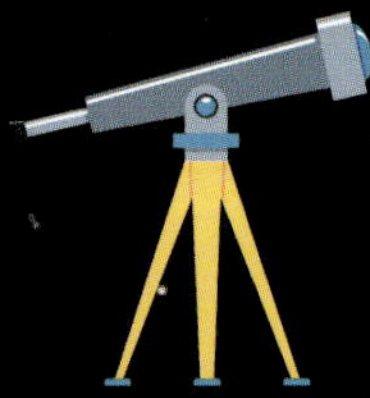

Telescopes are amazing inventions that allow us to see far out into space and discover new information about the stars, planets and other parts of our **solar system**.

Traditional telescopes have glass lenses that create magnified images. Very large telescopes are kept in buildings called *observatories*.

In 1609, famous astronomer, *Galileo*, was the first person to see mountains and **craters** on the moon through a telescope.

The Hubble Space Telescope is about the size of a school bus. It orbits Earth, sending images and information back to us. It can see much further into space than a regular telescope on Earth could.

Radio telescopes are used to record the radio waves of space objects, instead of images.

Is There Life Out There?

So far, no real evidence of life beyond our planet has been found, but many scientists believe we may not be alone in the Universe.

Most scientists believe that a planet would need air, water, and the right amount of heat and light, to be able to support life.

Scientists have sent radio messages into space, but so far there has been no response.

Mars used to be warmer and wetter than it is now, so could have supported life. Space probes have been sent there to search for signs of tiny living things, like **bacteria.**

There are thousands of other planets in our galaxy alone, so it's likely that at least some of them could contain life. However, most of them are too far away for us to study properly.

International Space Station (ISS)

The ISS is a large spacecraft in orbit around Earth. It is home to crews of astronauts and cosmonauts.

Scientists are using the space station to learn more about living and working in space.

Spacecraft are used to take astronauts and cosmonauts to and from the ISS, and to deliver supplies.

There is zero gravity on board the ISS, which means that everything floats, unless it is secured, including the crew!

The ISS orbits Earth every 90 minutes and the people living there experience 16 sunrises a day!

Satellites

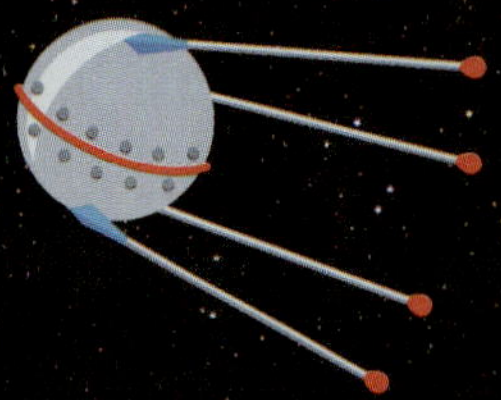

A satellite is something that orbits a planet or a star. The Moon is a satellite of the Earth and Earth is a satellite of the Sun.

There are currently over 2,000 active **artificial satellites** orbiting Earth.

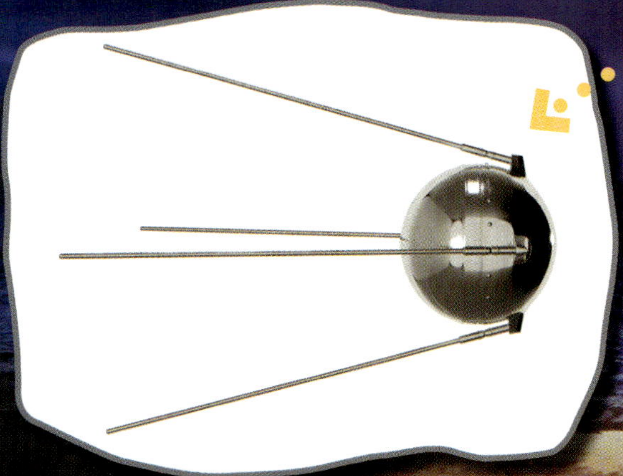

Sputnik 1 was the first artificial satellite to be launched into Earth's orbit, in October 1957.

Satellites are used for many purposes, including communication, **navigation,** and predicting weather.

Many satellites are powered by solar panels, which collect energy from sunlight.

What's Next?

There is so much of space left to be explored! Where will space travel take us next, and what will we discover along the way?

NASA is working on the *Space Launch System (SLS)*, their most powerful rocket yet. It should allow astronauts to travel deeper into space than ever before.

Space travel is very expensive, but scientists are working to create affordable and reusable spacccraft to allow more people to travel into space.

Glossary

artificial satellite – a man-made satellite that is launched into space by humans.

bacteria – also known as germs, are tiny living things that can only be seen using a microscope.

cargo – items or supplies carried by a vehicle.

cosmonaut – is a Russian or Soviet astronaut.

crater - a large hole in the ground, which has been caused by something hitting it, or by an explosion

Earth's atmosphere - layers of gases around the Earth, held in place by gravity.

meteorites – are rocks that have fallen to Earth from space.

navigation – to find your way from place to place.

orbit - the path taken by one object circling around another object in space.

retired – something that is no longer used (or someone who has stopped working).

solar system – the solar system contains all of the planets, dwarf planets, moons, and other objects that travel around the Sun.

Picture Credits

(abbreviations: t = top; b = bottom; m = middle; l = left; r = right; bg = background)

Shutterstock: Dima Zel 1bg, 2bg, 6bg; rangizzz 4bg; Asetta 4bl; Arkady Mazor 5r; Castleski 6l; solarseven 7tr; Kent Weakley 8bg; Crystal Eye Studio 9t; Sirko_Herr 10bg; Aleks49 10l; Digital Images Studio 11tl; Castleski 11bl; Paopano 12bg; Vadim Sadovski 12mr, 18bg, 24bg; AleksandrMorrisovich 14bg; Bill Anastasiou 14l; Andrew Barker 15bl; KeremGogus 16bg; Merlin74 17m; Tatiana Shepeleva 20bg; woverwolf 20l; Johan Swanepoel 20br; 3000ad 22bg; 3Dsculptor 23tl; d3verro 1tr, 3t, 4tr, 8t, 10tr, 14t, 16t, 20t, 22t; VikiVector 6t, 12tr, 16mr, 18tr, 24tr; Yindee (astronaut cartoons).

First published in Great Britain in 2022 by Hungry Tomato Ltd
F1, Old Bakery Studios, Blewetts Wharf, Malpas Road, Truro, Cornwall, TR1 1QH, UK

A CIP catalogue record for this book is available from the British Library

Published and Distributed in India by Scholastic India Pvt. Ltd.

ISBN 978-93-5471-931-8

This reprint edition : January 2025

Printed in India at Shree Maitrey Printech Pvt. Ltd., Noida